Nature fact file

Snakes

Barbara Taylor

Consultant: Michael Chinery

southwater

This edition published by Southwater

Distributed in the UK by
The Manning Partnership
251-253 London Road East
Batheaston, Bath BA1 7RL, UK
tel. (0044) 01225 852 727; fax. (0044) 01225 852 852

Distributed in the USA by Ottenheimer Publishing
5 Park Center Court, Suite 300
Owing Mills MD 2117-5001, USA
tel. (001) 410 902 9100; fax. (001) 410 902 7210

Distributed in Australia by Sandstone Publishing
Unit 1, 360 Norton Street, Leichhardt
New South Wales 2040, Australia
tel. (0061) 2 9560 7888; fax. (0061) 2 9560 7488

Distributed in New Zealand by Five Mile Press NZ
PO Box 33-1071
Takapuna, Auckland 9, New Zealand
tel. (0064) 9 4444 144; fax. (0064) 9 4444 518

Southwater is an imprint of Anness Publishing Limited
© 1998, 2000 Anness Publishing Limited

Publisher: Joanna Lorenz
Managing Editor: Gilly Cameron Cooper
Senior Editor: Nicole Pearson
Editor: Nicky Barber
Designer: Simon Wilder
Special Photography: Kim Taylor
Illustrations: Julian Baker, David Webb
Production Controller: Don Campaniello

PICTURE CREDITS
b=bottom, t=top, c=centre, l=left, r=right
Jane Burton/Warren Photographic: pages 29c, 40-41 and 48tr;
Bruce Coleman Ltd: pages 6bl, 8bl, 14br, 15r, 16tl, 17tl, 18tl,
19cr, 20cl, 20tr, 20br, 21tr, 21bl, 22br, 27br, 28t, 29b, 30br, 31t,
33cr, 33bl, 33r, 34bl, 36c, 37bl, 39br, 44cl, 44br, 46bl, 46br, 48tr,
48cr, 48b, 50cr, 50b, 53tr, 54bl, 56bl, 56cr, 59br, 60tr and 61b;
Ecoscene: pages 17cr and 59tl; Mary Evans Picture Library:
pages 45tr and 53br; FLPA: pages 11cr, 11cl, 16c, 18bl,
23tl, 23tr, 26tl, 26c, 31cr, 32-33, 35tr, 35bl, 38cr, 39t,
39bl, 40-41, 43tr, 45cl, 45br, 48cl, 51bl, 50-51, 52b, 52r,
55tl, 57bl and 60br; Holt Studios International: pages
22tl, 46tr and 58tl; Nature Photographers: page
30bc; NHPA: pages 7bl, 8tl, 9tr, 9bl, 11tl, 14tl, 18br,
19tl, 19br, 22bl, 23bl, 23br, 31cl, 36037, 37tr, 37cr,
38bl, 42cl, 47tl, 47cl, 47bl, 49cl, 49r, 50tl, 51t and
53c; Oxford Scientific Films: pages 6tc, 12-13, 24-
25, 42t, 43b and 56br; Planet Earth Pictures:
pages 28b, 32cl, 32br, 32tr, 38tr, 42br, 43c, 54tr,
54br, 55cr, 57cr, 60cl, 61tl and 61tr; Visual Arts
Library: pages 5br, 11br and 27bl; Zefa Pictures:
page 51br.

Special photography: Kim Taylor/Warren
Photographic: pages 1, 2, 3, 4-5, 7tr, 10bl, 10bc, 11tr,
12-13, 14-15, 16cl, 16bl, 24-25, 27tr, 29t, 31bl, 34tl,
34-35, 35cr, 36bl, 47r, 52cl, 56tr, 57t, 58b, 59c, 59bl,
62, 63 and 64.

No animals were harmed in the making of this
book.

Printed and bound in Hong Kong.
10 9 8 7 6 5 4 3 2 1

CON

T E N T S

long, thin, bendy body with no legs

tough scales protect the body and stop it drying out

SNAKE LIFE

Snakes are beautiful and secretive animals, and they are not nearly as dangerous as people think. They are a kind of reptile related to lizards, crocodiles and turtles. Altogether, there are about 2,700 different kinds of snake, but out of this number only 300 or so are able to kill people. In Europe or North America, you are more likely to be struck by lightning than to be bitten by a poisonous snake. All snakes have several things in common. They are long, thin animals with no legs, eyelids or outside ears. Their bodies are covered with tough, waterproof scales. Snakes have forked tongues for smelling and tasting the air. They are all flesh eaters and swallow their prey whole. Snakes have always had a special place in myths and legends, being used as symbols of both good and evil.

A SNAKE'S TAIL
It is often hard to tell where a snake's body ends and where its tail begins. The tail is the part behind a small opening called the cloaca, where the body wastes pass out. The snake narrows slightly at this point. The tail of a male snake is generally longer than that of the female.

tail, the part of the body that tapers off to a point

grass snake

SNAKE HEADS
Like this grass snake, most snakes have a definite head and neck. But in some snakes, one end of the body looks very much like the other end, except that the head has eyes, nostrils and a mouth, and the tail does not!

FORKED TONGUES

Snakes and some lizards are the only animals with forked tongues. A snake flicks its tongue in and out of its mouth to taste and smell the air. This gives the snake a picture of what is around it. A snake does this every few seconds if it is hunting or if there is danger nearby. The tongue will not sting if it touches your skin. The snake is just collecting information about you.

rattlesnake

Colombian rainbow boa

SCALY ARMOUR

A snake's skin is hidden under a covering of tough scales. The scales grow out of the skin and usually hide the skin from view. However, after a big meal, the scaly skin stretches so that the skin becomes visible between the scales. A snake's scales protect its body while allowing it to stretch, coil and bend. If you touch a snake, you will feel that the scales are dry. Some snakes have rough scales, whilst others have smooth ones.

Did you know? A boa squeezes its prey to death in its coils.

red-tailed boa

Did you know? Snakes never feel slimy to the touch.

MEDUSA

An ancient Greek myth tells the story of the Medusa, a monster with snakes for hair. Anyone who looked at her was turned to stone. Perseus managed to avoid this fate by using his polished shield to look only at the monster's reflection. He cut off the Medusa's head with his sword and carried it home, dripping with blood. As each drop touched the earth, it turned into a snake called a viper.

Did you know? Most snakes lay eggs but some give birth to baby snakes.

eye has no eyelid

forked tongue

SHAPES AND SIZES

Can you imagine a snake so big that it could stretch all the way from the ground to the roof of a three-storey house? The reticulated python is this big. The biggest snakes have thick, powerful bodies that measure nearly a metre round. Other snakes are as thin as a pencil and small enough to fit into the palm of your hand. Snakes also have different shapes to suit their different environments. Sea snakes have flat bodies and tails like oars to help them push against the water and move forwards. Burrowing snakes have rounded, tube-shaped bodies to help them slide easily through the soil. Pythons and vipers have fairly short tails, while the tails of some tree snakes are longer than their bodies.

THICK AND THIN

Vipers mostly have thick bodies with much thinner, short tails. They are not very long snakes. The bags of poison on either side of a viper's head take up a lot of space, so the head is large and broad. It is often a triangular shape.

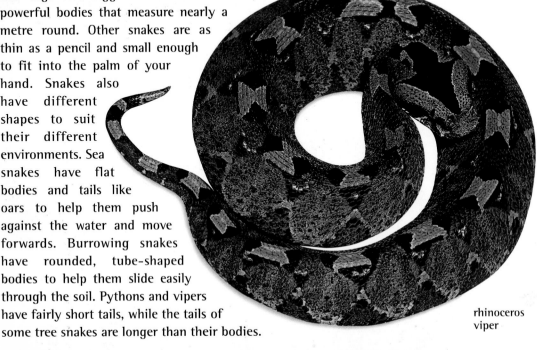

rhinoceros viper

LONG AND THIN

Tree snakes are often long and thin in shape, to help them slide through leaves and along branches. Even their heads are long and pointed. The head of a tree snake is also very light so that it does not weigh the snake down as it reaches out for the next branch. The long tail of a tree snake coils around branches to help it grip tightly as it climbs.

green tree snake

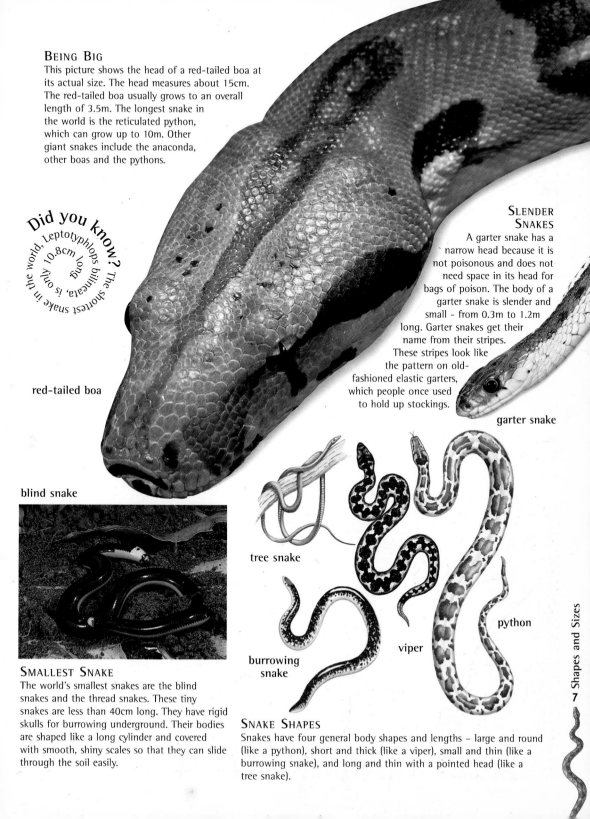

BEING BIG

This picture shows the head of a red-tailed boa at its actual size. The head measures about 15cm. The red-tailed boa usually grows to an overall length of 3.5m. The longest snake in the world is the reticulated python, which can grow up to 10m. Other giant snakes include the anaconda, other boas and the pythons.

Did you know? The shortest snake in the world, Leptotyphlops bilineata, is only 10.8cm long.

SLENDER SNAKES

A garter snake has a narrow head because it is not poisonous and does not need space in its head for bags of poison. The body of a garter snake is slender and small - from 0.3m to 1.2m long. Garter snakes get their name from their stripes. These stripes look like the pattern on old-fashioned elastic garters, which people once used to hold up stockings.

garter snake

red-tailed boa

blind snake

tree snake

burrowing snake

viper

python

SMALLEST SNAKE

The world's smallest snakes are the blind snakes and the thread snakes. These tiny snakes are less than 40cm long. They have rigid skulls for burrowing underground. Their bodies are shaped like a long cylinder and covered with smooth, shiny scales so that they can slide through the soil easily.

SNAKE SHAPES

Snakes have four general body shapes and lengths – large and round (like a python), short and thick (like a viper), small and thin (like a burrowing snake), and long and thin with a pointed head (like a tree snake).

egg-eating
snake

STRETCHY STOMACH
The big lump inside this snake is a whole egg. Luckily, the throat and gut of the snake are so elastic that the thin body of a snake can stretch wide enough to eat its large meal. The throat and first part of the gut are also very muscular, to help force food right down into the snake's stomach. The egg is broken on the way down.

HOW SNAKES WORK

A snake has a stretched-out inside to match its long, thin outside. The backbone extends along the whole body with hundreds of ribs joined to it. There is not much room for organs, such as the heart, lungs, kidneys and liver, so these organs are thin shapes to fit inside the snake's body. Many snakes have only one lung. The stomach and gut are very stretchy so that they can hold large meals. When a snake is swallowing large animals, it pushes the opening of the windpipe up from the floor of the mouth in order to keep breathing. Snakes are cold-blooded, which means that their body temperature is the same as their surroundings. This is why most snakes live in warm places where the temperature is high enough for them to stay active both day and night.

right lung is very long and thin and does the work of two lungs

liver is very long and thin

flexible tail bone, which extends from the back bone

banded rattlesnake

INSIDE A SNAKE
This diagram shows what a male snake looks like inside and the position of its main organs. The organs are arranged to fit the snake's long body shape. In most animals, paired organs, such as the kidneys and lungs, are the same size and placed opposite each other. But as snakes have developed over time, the left lung has disappeared altogether in many species.

WARMING UP AND COOLING DOWN
Like all snakes, the banded rattlesnake is an ectotherm. This means that it is cold-blooded. In order to warm up or cool down, it has to move from sun to shade. The word ectothermic means outside heat because the main source of a snake's body-heat is outside its body.

rectum through which waste is passed to the cloaca

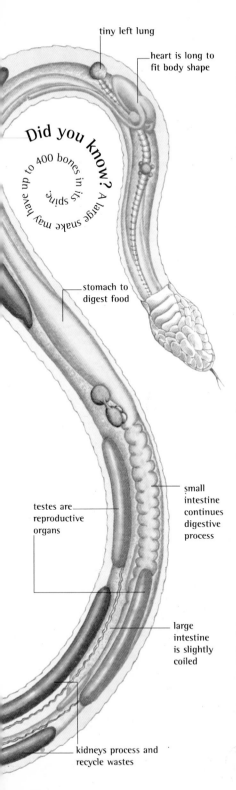

tiny left lung

heart is long to fit body shape

Did you know? A large snake may have up to 400 bones in its spine.

stomach to digest food

small intestine continues digestive process

testes are reproductive organs

large intestine is slightly coiled

kidneys process and recycle wastes

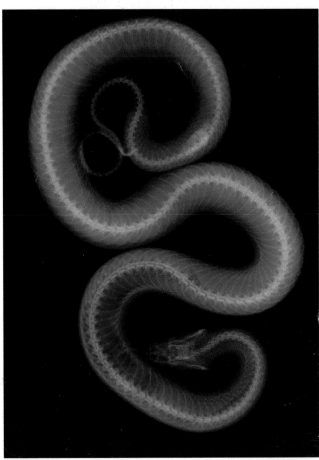

SNAKE BONES

Look at this X-ray of a grass snake and you will see the bones that make up its skeleton. There are no arm, leg, shoulder or hip bones. A few other snakes do have very tiny hip and back leg bones, but these are not used for walking. If you look carefully, you will see that the ribs do not extend into the tail. Snake bones are delicate and easily damaged.

SKELETON

A snake's skeleton is made up of a skull and a long backbone with ribs arching out from it. The free ends of the ribs are linked by muscles, forming a tube of bone and muscle that protects the snake's organs. The loose joints in a snake's backbone allow it to bend and coil its body.

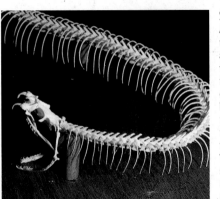

viper skeleton

A SCALY SKIN

HORNED SNAKE

As its name suggests, the European nose-horned viper has a strange horn on its nose. The horn is made up of small scales that lie over a bony or fleshy lump sticking out at the end of the nose. No one knows what the horn is used for. Other snakes, such as shovel-nosed snakes, have large scales on the ends of their noses, which they use for burrowing in the ground.

A snake's scales are extra-thick pieces of skin. They work like a suit of armour to protect the snake from bumps, knocks and scrapes as it moves about. They also allow the skin to stretch when the snake moves or feeds. Scales are usually made of a horny substance, called keratin, which forms your hair and nails, as well as the claws, hoofs and feathers of other animals. Every part of a snake's body is covered by a layer of scales, including the eyes. The clear, bubble-like scale that protects each eye is called a brille or spectacle. The scales of most snakes also contain the pigments that give snakes their many colours. Every so often a snake grows a shiny new skin underneath its old one. Then it wriggles out of the dead skin.

nose-horned viper

SCUTES

Most snakes have a row of broad scales, called scutes, underneath their bodies. The scutes go across a snake's body from side to side, and end where the tail starts. Scutes help snakes to grip the ground, like the tyres of a caterpillar tractor. Many burrowing and water snakes do not have scutes.

WARNING RATTLE

The rattlesnake has a number of hollow tail-tips that make a dry, buzzing sound when shaken. The snake uses this sound to warn enemies to keep away. Every time a rattlesnake sheds its skin a section at the end of the tail is left behind, adding another piece to the rattle.

rattlesnake's rattle

corn snake's scutes

SKIN SCALES

When a snake's skin is stretched, the scales pull apart so that you can see the skin between the scales. The scales grow out of the top layer of the skin, called the epidermis. There are different kinds of scales. Keeled scales may help snakes to grip surfaces, or break up a snake's outline for camouflage. Smooth scales make it easier for the snake to squeeze through tight spaces.

Look closely at the rough scales of the puff adder (left) and you will see a raised ridge, or keel, sticking up in the middle of each one.

Did you know? Most snakes get their colours from pigments in the scales.

corn snake's scales

The wart snake (right) uses its scales to hold on to its food. Its rough scales help the snake to keep a firm grip on slippery fish until it can swallow them. The wart snake's scales do not overlap.

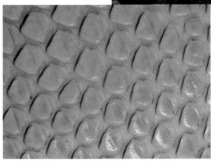

ETERNAL YOUTH

A poem written in the Middle East about 3,700 years ago tells a story about why snakes can shed their skins. The hero of the poem is Gilgamesh (shown here holding a captured lion). He finds a magic plant that will make a person young again. While he is washing at a pool, a snake eats the plant. Since then, according to the poem, snakes have been able to shed their skins and become young again. But people have never found the plant of eternal youth – which is why they always grow old and die.

The green scales and stretched blue skin (left) belong to a boa. These smooth scales help the boa to slide easily through leafy branches. Burrowing snakes also have smooth scales so that they can slip through the soil.

Did you know? The hairy bush viper has pointed scales with curled tips, making it look hairy

A Scaly Skin

11

1 READY TO SHED
A snake sheds its outer layer of scaly skin when a new layer of skin and scales has grown underneath the old one. In the days before it peels, a snake is sluggish and bad-tempered, and its colours become dull. Its eyes turn cloudy or blue as the eye coverings gradually become loose. About 24 hours before moulting, the eyes clear again.

A NEW SKIN

One of the most amazing things about snakes is the almost magical way they wriggle out of their old, tight skin to reveal a bright, new, shiny skin underneath. Unlike humans, who shed little flakes of old skin and grow new skin all the time, snakes shed their worn-out skin and scales in one piece. This process is called moulting or sloughing. Snakes only moult when a new layer of skin and scales has grown underneath the old skin. Adult snakes slough their skin up to about six times a year.

2 THE FIRST SPLIT
The paper-thin layer of outer skin and scales first starts to peel away around the mouth. The snake rubs its jaws and chin against rocks or rough bark, and crawls through plants. This helps to push off the loose layer of skin.

Did you know? A baby snake may shed its skin when it is only a few days old

3 PEELING OFF

The outer layer of skin gradually peels back from the head over the rest of the body. The snake slides out of its old skin, which comes off inside-out. It is rather like taking hold of a long sock at the top and peeling it down over your leg and foot!

Did you know? Female snakes often shed their skin just before giving birth.

4 SHEDDING SKIN

A snake usually takes several hours to shed its whole skin. The old skin is moist and supple soon after shedding, but gradually dries out to become crinkly and rather brittle. The moulted skin is an exact copy of the snake's scale pattern. It is very delicate. If you hold a moulted snake skin up to the light, you will notice that it is almost see-through.

5 THE OLD SKIN

A shed skin is longer than the snake itself. This is because the skin stretches as the snake wriggles free. It is not coloured but may have traces of the snake's pattern left on it. The snake's new skin is brightly coloured and shiny, with a well-marked pattern.

SNAKES ON THE MOVE

For animals without legs, snakes move around very well. They can glide over or under the ground, climb trees and swim gracefully through water. A few snakes can even parachute through the air. Snakes are not speedy animals, however. Most move at about 3kph. With their bendy backbones, snakes have a flexible, wavy movement. They push themselves along using muscles joined to their ribs. The scales on their skin also grip surfaces to help with movement. Snakes move in four main ways – wriggling from side to side, crawling straight forwards, moving like a concertina and sidewinding. The type of movement depends on the size of the snake and, most importantly, on its surroundings.

Did you know? A person can walk faster than most snakes can move.

corn snake

S-SHAPED MOVER

Most snakes move in an S-shaped path. They push the side curves of their bodies backwards against the surface they are travelling on or through. The muscular waves of the snake's body hit surrounding objects and the whole body is pushed forward from there. A snake track in sand has small heaps on the outside edges of the curves where the snake has pushed hard against the sand.

banded sea snake

SWIMMING SNAKE

The startling stripes of the banded sea snake stand out as it glides effortlessly through the water. Snakes always swim using S-shaped movements. Instead of pushing against the ground, a sea snake pushes against the water. A sea snake's tail is flattened from side to side to give it extra power, like the oar on a rowing boat.

CONCERTINA SNAKE

The green whip snake moves with an action rather like a concertina. The concertina is played by squeezing forwards and backwards. The green whip snake moves by gripping on to a surface with the back part of its body while stretching the front part forwards. Then the front half holds on while the back half is drawn up to meet it.

green whip snake

Peringuey's viper

SIDEWINDING

This way of moving is used by snakes that live on loose sand. The snake anchors its head and tail in the sand and moves the middle part of its body sideways. Then it grips with the middle part of the body and moves its head and tail sideways, winding along at an angle of 45° to the direction of travel.

Did you know? The fastest land snake is the black mamba, moving at up to 11 kph.

HOW SNAKES MOVE

Most land snakes move in four different ways, depending on the type of terrain they are crossing and the type of snake.

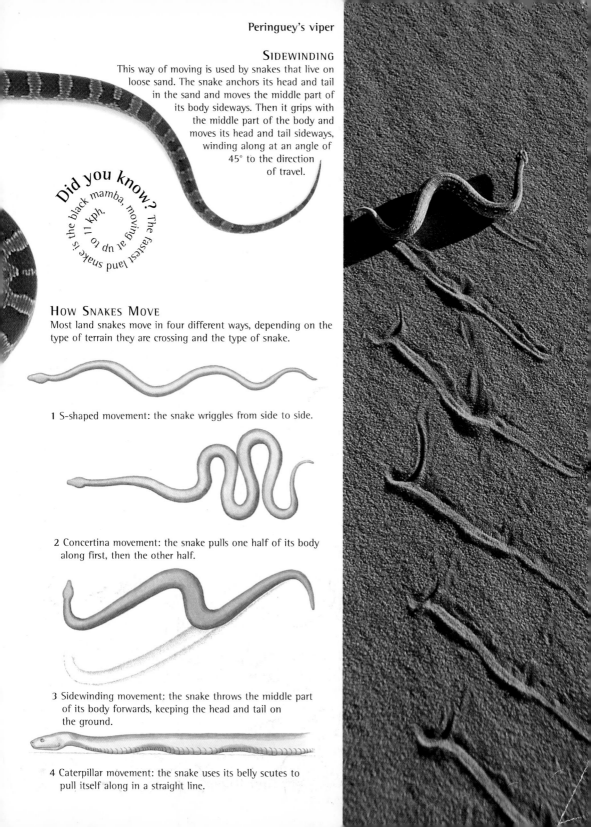

1 S-shaped movement: the snake wriggles from side to side.

2 Concertina movement: the snake pulls one half of its body along first, then the other half.

3 Sidewinding movement: the snake throws the middle part of its body forwards, keeping the head and tail on the ground.

4 Caterpillar movement: the snake uses its belly scutes to pull itself along in a straight line.

EYESIGHT
This snake seems to have a glassy stare because it has no eyelids to cover its eyes. Eyesight varies in snakes, but even those with good sight probably detect movement rather than the shape or form of objects. The snakes with the best eyesight are tree snakes, such as this green mamba, and day hunters such as garter snakes.

SNAKE SENSES

To find prey and avoid enemies, snakes rely more on their senses of smell, taste and touch than on sight and hearing. Some snakes can see well – tree snakes for example – but others, such as burrowing snakes, are almost blind. Snakes have no outside ears or eardrums, but they do have one earbone joined to the jaw. They can pick up sound vibrations through the ground and probably some low sounds travelling through the air. As well as their ordinary senses, snakes also have some special ones. They are almost the only animals to taste and smell with their tongues. There are also some snakes, such as pit vipers, that can sense the heat given off by their prey through pits on the sides of their faces. No other animal can do this.

green tree python

NIGHT HUNTERS
At night, the eyes of the horned viper open wide to let in as much light as possible (*above*). The horned viper is a night hunter. During the day, its pupils close down to narrow slits to protect the eyes from bright light (*below*).

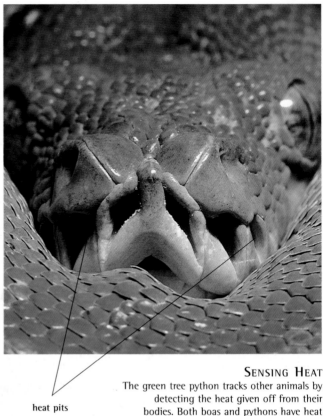

heat pits

SENSING HEAT
The green tree python tracks other animals by detecting the heat given off from their bodies. Both boas and pythons have heat holes along the lips. These heat sensors are lined with nerves. They allow a snake to find and kill prey in total darkness.

THE FORKED TONGUE

When snakes want to investigate their surroundings, they flick out their tongues to taste the air. The forked tongue picks up tiny chemical particles of scent from the air or off the ground.

HEARING

The cobra cannot hear the music played by the snake charmer. It follows the movements of the pipe and rises up as it prepares to defend itself. Snakes are not deaf, though. The lower jaw picks up vibrations carried through the ground and passes them on to the small ear bone. From these vibrations, a snake can tell if an animal is coming towards it or going away, and if the animal is big or small.

black-tailed rattlesnake

JACOBSON'S ORGAN

As a snake draws its tongue back into its mouth, it presses the forked tip into the two openings of the Jacobson's organ. This organ is in the roof of the mouth and it analyses tastes and smells. Information from the Jacobson's organ tells the snake about food, predators, mates and other important things.

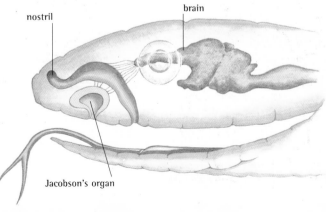

nostril

brain

Jacobson's organ

FOOD AND HUNTING

All snakes are hunters, catching and killing other animals. However, snakes eat different foods and hunt in different ways depending on their size, their species and where they live. Some snakes eat a wide variety of food, while others have a more specialized diet. Thread snakes eat only slugs and snails, and egg-eating snakes eat only the eggs of birds and reptiles. A few snakes, such as the king snake, hunt and eat other snakes. A snake has to make the most of each meal because it moves fairly slowly and does not get the chance to catch prey very often. Luckily, a snake's body works at a slow rate so it can go for months without eating. A snake uses its senses to detect other animals and, instead of hunting, many snakes simply lie in wait for their prey to come to them.

rat snake

TREE HUNTERS
A rat snake grasps the body of a baby bluebird between its jaws and begins the process of digestion. Rat snakes are good climbers and often slither up trees in search of baby birds, eggs or squirrels.

Did you know?
Some Cuban boas feed on bats

tentacled snake

TRICKY LURE
The Australasian death adder has a brightly coloured tail tip that looks just like a worm. It uses its tail tip as a lure to trick prey. The adder wriggles the 'worm' to lure lizards, birds and small mammals to come within range of its deadly, poisonous fangs.

FISHY FOOD
Like many snakes, the tentacled snake lives on fish. Tentacled snakes probably hide among plants in the water and grab fish as they swim past. Sea snakes have narrow heads and necks to search out fish that are hidden among rocks and coral, or down mud burrows. These snakes catch mainly slow-moving fish, or fish that are resting at night.

death adder

African egg-eater

EGG-EATERS

Snakes eat eggs because they are a rich source of food – and they do not fight back! The snake first checks the egg with its tongue to make sure it is fresh. Then it swallows the egg whole. It uses the pointed ends of the bones in its backbone to crack the eggshell. The snake swallows the yolk and white of the egg, then coughs up the crushed eggshell.

SURPRISE ATTACK

Lunch for this gaboon viper is a mouse! The gaboon viper hides among dry leaves on the forest floor. Its colouring and markings make it very difficult to spot. It waits for a small animal to pass by, then grabs hold of its prey in a surprise attack. Many other snakes that hunt by day also ambush their prey.

Did you know? Sometimes a snake coughs up its prey – alive!

gaboon viper

smooth snake

SNAKE EATS SNAKE

This smooth snake is eating an asp viper. The viper fits neatly inside the body of the smooth snake. This makes it easier to swallow than animals that are different shapes. Although the viper is poisonous, the smooth snake is not affected by the viper's poison. King snakes can eat poisonous rattlesnakes without being harmed, too.

TEETH AND JAWS

Most snakes have short, sharp teeth that curve backwards. Snakes' teeth are good for gripping and holding prey, but not for chopping or chewing it into smaller pieces. The teeth are not very strong, and often get broken, so they are continually being replaced. Poisonous snakes have some teeth that are much larger than the others. These teeth are called fangs and they may be in the front or the back of the mouth. When the snake bites, poison flows down the fangs to paralyse the prey and break down its body. All snakes swallow their prey head-first and whole, even when the victim's body is bigger than the snake's. Special loose jaws allow the snake to open its mouth wider than any other animal. The jaws 'walk' over the prey to force it down the snake's throat.

BACK FANGS
A few poisonous snakes, such as this African boomslang, have fangs at the back of their mouths. Poison runs down grooves in the fangs. The boomslang is digging its fangs hard into the flesh of a chameleon to get enough poison inside.

boomslang

OPEN WIDE
An eyelash viper opens its mouth as wide as possible to scare off an enemy. You can see that its fangs are folded back against the roof of the mouth. If the viper were to attack its enemy, the fangs would swing quickly forwards.

FOLDING FANGS
There are two main kinds of snake with fangs at the front of the mouth – vipers and elapid snakes. Snakes in the viper family have long fangs that can be folded back. When a viper strikes at its prey, the fangs swing forward so that they stick out in front of the mouth. The fangs inject poison deep into the victim.

 Movable fangs

viper skull

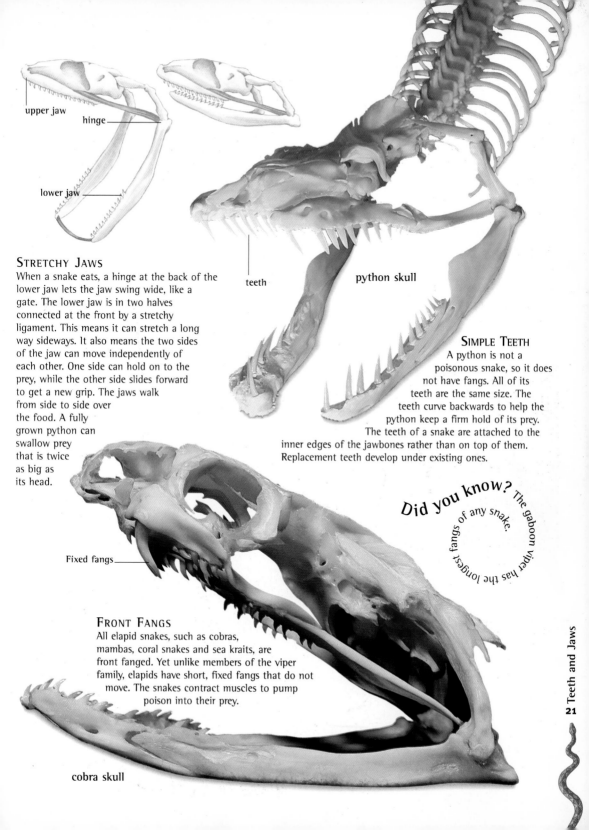

upper jaw

hinge

lower jaw

STRETCHY JAWS

When a snake eats, a hinge at the back of the lower jaw lets the jaw swing wide, like a gate. The lower jaw is in two halves connected at the front by a stretchy ligament. This means it can stretch a long way sideways. It also means the two sides of the jaw can move independently of each other. One side can hold on to the prey, while the other side slides forward to get a new grip. The jaws walk from side to side over the food. A fully grown python can swallow prey that is twice as big as its head.

teeth

python skull

SIMPLE TEETH

A python is not a poisonous snake, so it does not have fangs. All of its teeth are the same size. The teeth curve backwards to help the python keep a firm hold of its prey. The teeth of a snake are attached to the inner edges of the jawbones rather than on top of them. Replacement teeth develop under existing ones.

Did you know? The gaboon viper has the longest fangs of any snake.

Fixed fangs

FRONT FANGS

All elapid snakes, such as cobras, mambas, coral snakes and sea kraits, are front fanged. Yet unlike members of the viper family, elapids have short, fixed fangs that do not move. The snakes contract muscles to pump poison into their prey.

cobra skull

American racer

STRANGLERS AND POISONERS

Some snakes grab their prey and swallow it alive. However, most snakes kill their prey before eating it. Snakes need to overpower their prey quickly. If a victim fights back, a snake risks injury to its delicate body. Snakes have two main ways of killing, by using poison or by squeezing their prey to death. Snakes that squeeze are called constrictors. They stop their prey from breathing, but they do not crush their bodies. Victims die from suffocation or shock. To swallow living or dead prey, a snake opens its jaws wide. Lots of slimy saliva helps the meal to slide down. After eating, a snake yawns widely to put its jaws back into place. Digestion may take several days, or even weeks, but happens faster when the snake's body is warm.

BIG MOUTHFUL
This American racer is trying to swallow a living frog, but the frog is not too keen on the idea! It has puffed up its body with air to make it more difficult for the snake to swallow. Sometimes, a snake eats a frog feet first and squeezes the air out through the frog's mouth.

fer-de-lance

copperhead

AT FULL STRETCH
This fer-de-lance snake is at full stretch to swallow its huge meal – a whole agouti. The fer-de-lance is probably the most dangerous snake in South America. It is a large pit viper that kills with poison.

SWALLOWING A MEAL
A copperhead holds on to its dead prey – a mouse. Copperheads are the most widespread poisonous snakes in eastern North America. They often live near homes, but they have weak poison and rarely bite people. As well as mice, they eat frogs, toads and salamanders.

rock python

Did you know?
Pythons can kill and eat leopards.

spotted
python

KILLING TIME
A crocodile is slowly squeezed to death by a rock
python. The time it takes for a constricting snake to
kill its prey depends on the size of the prey and how
strong it is. Small animals may die in just a few
seconds. Large prey may struggle for much longer.

Did you know?
King cobras sometimes kill Indian elephants by biting them on the trunk.

COILED KILLER
The spotted python sinks
its sharp teeth into its
victim. Once it has a firm grip
it throws two or more coils
around the victim's body. Each
time the animal breathes out,
the snake tightens its grip.
Eventually, the animal cannot
breathe in at all.

carpet python

BREATHING TUBE
An African python displays its breathing tube.
Swallowing prey can take a long time. With a
mouth full of food, a snake could have a
problem breathing. So, the windpipe moves to
the front of the mouth. This means that air can
get to and from the lungs as the snake eats.

HEAD-FIRST
The hind legs of a whiptail wallaby are the last thing to
disappear inside this carpet python's body. Snakes usually try
to swallow their prey head-first so that legs, wings or scales
fold back. This helps the victim to slide into the snake's
stomach more easily.

Stranglers and Poisoners

23

1 LOOKING FOR FOOD
Rat snakes feed on rats, mice, voles, lizards, birds and eggs. Many of them hunt at night. They are good climbers and can even go up trees with smooth bark and no branches. Rat snakes find their prey by following a scent trail or waiting to ambush an animal.

LET'S DO LUNCH!

This rat snake is using its strong coils to kill a vole for its supper. Rodents, such as voles and rats, are a rat snake's favourite food. After using its senses to find the vole, the snake slides near enough for a quick strike. With the vole held tightly in its sharp teeth, the rat snake coils around its body. It squeezes hard to stop the vole breathing. When the vole is dead, the rat snake opens its jaws very wide and swallows its furry meal head-first.

2 TEETH AND COILS
When the rat snake is near enough to its prey, it strikes quickly. Its sharp teeth sink into the victim's body to stop it running or flying away. The snake then loops its coils around the victim as fast as possible, before the animal can bite or scratch to defend itself.

3 A TIGHT SQUEEZE
Each time the victim breathes out, the rat snake squeezes a little harder around its rib cage. This stops the animal from breathing in again. Breathing becomes more and more difficult as the rat snake tightens its coils. Soon the prey cannot breathe at all and dies from suffocation.

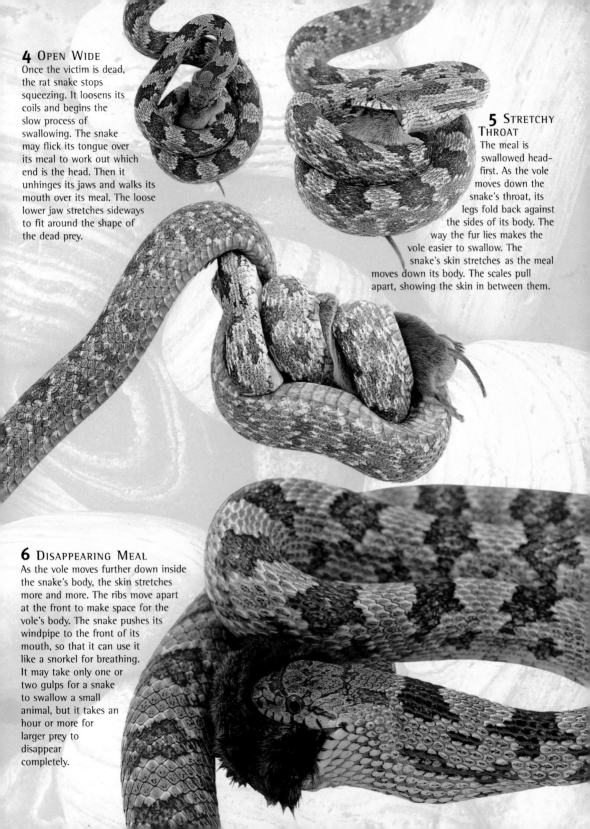

4 OPEN WIDE
Once the victim is dead, the rat snake stops squeezing. It loosens its coils and begins the slow process of swallowing. The snake may flick its tongue over its meal to work out which end is the head. Then it unhinges its jaws and walks its mouth over its meal. The loose lower jaw stretches sideways to fit around the shape of the dead prey.

5 STRETCHY THROAT
The meal is swallowed head-first. As the vole moves down the snake's throat, its legs fold back against the sides of its body. The way the fur lies makes the vole easier to swallow. The snake's skin stretches as the meal moves down its body. The scales pull apart, showing the skin in between them.

6 DISAPPEARING MEAL
As the vole moves further down inside the snake's body, the skin stretches more and more. The ribs move apart at the front to make space for the vole's body. The snake pushes its windpipe to the front of its mouth, so that it can use it like a snorkel for breathing. It may take only one or two gulps for a snake to swallow a small animal, but it takes an hour or more for larger prey to disappear completely.

POISONOUS SNAKES

Less than a quarter of all snakes – about 700 species – are poisonous, and only about half of these poisonous species can kill people. Snake poison is called venom. Venom is very useful for snakes because it allows them to kill without having to fight a long battle against their prey. This means that poisonous snakes are less likely to be wounded by bigger animals with sharp teeth and claws. Some snake venom also works on the body of the prey, softening it and making it easier for the snake to digest. There are two main kinds of snake venom. One type attacks the blood and muscles. The other attacks the nervous system, stopping the heart and lungs from working. A poisonous snake stores venom in a bag in its head and injects it into prey through large teeth, called fangs.

POISONOUS BITE
A copperhead gets ready to strike. Poisonous snakes use their sharp fangs to inject a lethal cocktail of chemicals into their prey. The death of victims often occurs in seconds or minutes, depending on the size of the prey and where it was bitten.

WARNING COLOURS
The brightly coloured stripes of coral snakes warn predators that these snakes are very poisonous. Birds and other predators soon learn to leave them alone. There are more than 50 species of coral snake, all with similar patterns. But predators remember the basic pattern and avoid all coral snakes.

spitting cobra

VENOM SPIT
Spitting cobras use their venom for attack and defence. They have an opening in their fangs to squirt venom into an enemy's face. They aim at the eyes, and the venom can cause pain and blindness.

coral snake

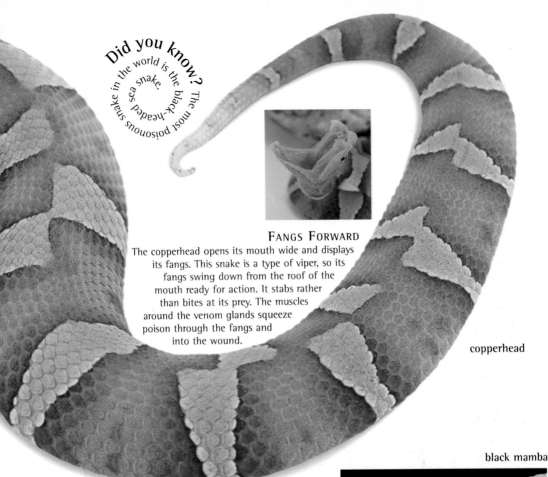

FANGS FORWARD

The copperhead opens its mouth wide and displays its fangs. This snake is a type of viper, so its fangs swing down from the roof of the mouth ready for action. It stabs rather than bites at its prey. The muscles around the venom glands squeeze poison through the fangs and into the wound.

copperhead

black mamba

BIBLE SNAKE

At the beginning of the Bible, a snake is the cause of problems in the Garden of Eden. God told Adam and Eve never to eat fruit from the tree of knowledge of good and evil. However, the snake persuaded Eve to eat the fruit. It told Eve that the fruit would make her as clever as God. Eve gave some fruit to Adam too. As a punishment, Adam and Eve had to leave the garden of Eden and lose the gift of eternal life.

MILKING VENOM

Venom is collected by making a black mamba bite through the top of a jar. The venom is used to make a medicine called antivenin. It can stop people dying from snake bites.

green bush viper

VIPERS

From adders and asps to rattlesnakes and copperheads, vipers are the most efficient poisonous snakes in the world. Their long fangs can inject venom deep into a victim. The venom acts mainly on the blood and muscles of the prey. Vipers usually have short, thick bodies and triangular heads covered with many small scales. All the scales are ridged. There are two main groups of vipers. Typical vipers and adders live in Europe, Asia and Africa. Pit vipers, such as rattlesnakes, live in the Americas and southern Asia. The main difference between the two groups is that pit vipers have large heat pits on the face and other vipers do not. Most vipers give birth to fully developed, or live, young.

TREE VIPER

The green bush viper lives in tropical forests, mainly in the trees. Its colouring means that it is well camouflaged against the green leaves. It lies in wait for its prey and then kills it with a quick bite. Once the prey has been caught, the snake must hold tight to stop it falling out of the tree.

puff adder

BALLOON SNAKE

When threatened, the puff adder swells up like a long balloon. It does this by taking a lot of air into its lungs. Being larger makes it look more dangerous. Many of the true vipers can swell up in this way. Puff adders also hiss with a loud sound that can be heard some distance away.

rattlesnake

FEARSOME FANGS

This rattlesnake is exploring its surroundings with its forked tongue. When the rattlesnake strikes at its prey, its mouth opens wide. The long, hinged fangs swing forward and lock into place. The viper stabs its prey to give it a quick injection of powerful venom, then lets go. The prey soon dies, so there is no need for the snake to hold on to it. If the prey does manage to move away, the snake can easily track it down.

HEAT DETECTORS

This beautiful Sumatran pit viper has a large heat pit on each side of its head, between the nostril and the eye. The heat pit is larger than the nostril. It can detect the heat given off by warm-blooded prey. By turning the head from side to side, a pit viper can work out the direction of its prey. When both pits receive the same amount of warmth, the prey is straight ahead. Pit vipers can also work out how far away their prey is, which helps them to strike accurately.

SLOW SNAKE

Asp vipers are slow-moving snakes. They are active both by day and by night. Their main sources of food are mice, lizards and baby birds in their nests. The asp viper does not usually kill people, but its bite is painful.

Sumatran pit viper

DEFENCE

Most snakes, especially baby snakes and snake eggs, are eaten by a wide range of animals. Snakes provide food for birds of prey, such as eagles. They are also hunted by predators such as foxes, racoons, mongooses, baboons, crocodiles, frogs and even other snakes. If they are in danger, snakes usually prefer to hide or escape. Many come out to hunt at night, when it is more difficult for predators to catch them. If they cannot escape, snakes often make themselves look big and fierce, hiss loudly or strike at their enemies. Some pretend to be dead. Giving off a horrible smell is another good way of getting rid of an enemy! Many snakes will twist into a ball or figure of eight, smearing the strong-smelling substance over their body. Poisonous snakes defend themselves with their venom, but they try to avoid fighting in case they get hurt.

SMELLY SNAKE

The poisonous cottonmouth is named after the white colour of the inside of its mouth. It opens its mouth to threaten enemies. If a cottonmouth is attacked, it can also give off a strong-smelling liquid from near the tail. By swishing its tail from side to side, the cottonmouth can spray this smelly liquid up to 1m away.

EAGLE ENEMY

The short-toed eagle uses its powerful toes to catch snakes on open hillsides. It tears apart a large snake with its sharp beak and eats it on the ground. It can carry small snakes back to the nest to feed its chicks.

SCARY MOUTH

Like many snakes, this vine snake opens its mouth very wide to startle predators. The inside of the mouth is a bright red colour. If the predator does not go away, the snake will give a poisonous bite with the fangs at the back of the mouth. The open mouth is a warning message saying 'Go away or I will bite you!'

vine snake

cottonmouth

PLAYING DEAD

This grass snake knows that most predators prefer healthy, living prey. So it protects itself by pretending to be dead. Many other snakes also do this. They roll on to their backs, open their mouths and keep quite still. When the danger has passed, they come back to life again.

grass snake

cobra

hognose snake

DRAMATIC DISPLAY

The hognose snake of North America is harmless, but makes itself look dangerous in a dramatic display. First, it flattens its neck to make a hood. Then it hisses loudly and strikes towards the enemy. If that does not work, the hognose wriggles and smears itself with smelly scent. Finally, it rolls over and pretends to be dead.

HIDDEN SNAKE

The best defence for many snakes is to avoid being seen at all. The horned viper buries itelf. Its scales keep the sand from piling up and covering the eyes when the snake is buried.

horned viper

LOOKING LARGER

This cobra is rearing up and spreading its hood wide to make itself look as big and frightening as possible. This helps to scare away predators and also makes the cobra look too big for other animals to swallow.

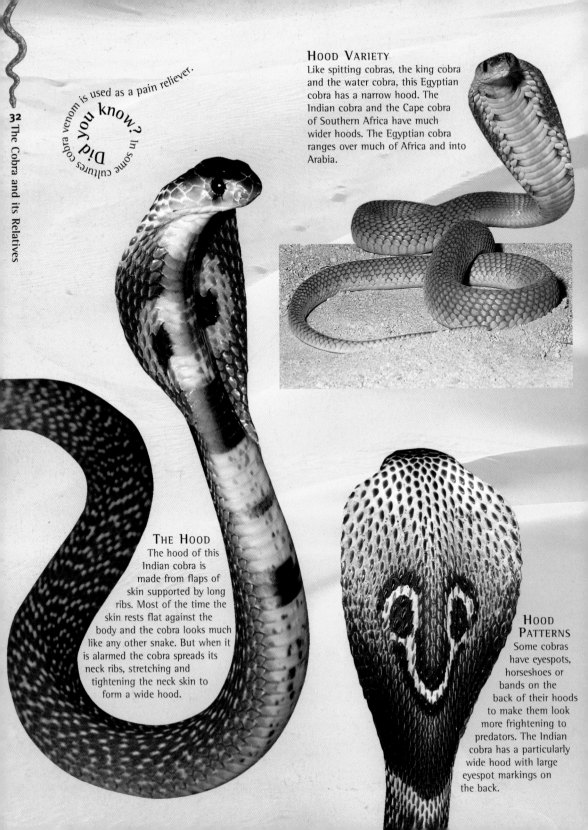

Did you know? In some cultures cobra venom is used as a pain reliever.

HOOD VARIETY
Like spitting cobras, the king cobra and the water cobra, this Egyptian cobra has a narrow hood. The Indian cobra and the Cape cobra of Southern Africa have much wider hoods. The Egyptian cobra ranges over much of Africa and into Arabia.

THE HOOD
The hood of this Indian cobra is made from flaps of skin supported by long ribs. Most of the time the skin rests flat against the body and the cobra looks much like any other snake. But when it is alarmed the cobra spreads its neck ribs, stretching and tightening the neck skin to form a wide hood.

HOOD PATTERNS
Some cobras have eyespots, horseshoes or bands on the back of their hoods to make them look more frightening to predators. The Indian cobra has a particularly wide hood with large eyespot markings on the back.

THE COBRA AND ITS RELATIVES

Cobras are very dramatic and very poisonous snakes. They have short, fixed fangs at the front of their mouths. Some cobras can squirt their deadly venom at their enemies. Cobra venom works mainly on the nervous system, causing breathing or heart problems. Cobras are members of the elapid snake family, which includes the mambas of Africa, the coral snakes of the Americas and all the poisonous snakes of Australia, such as tiger snakes.

LARGE COBRA
The king cobra is the largest of all venomous snakes, growing to a length of 5.5 m. It is shy and prefers to keep well away from people. King cobras are the only snakes known to build a nest. The female lays 20 to 40 eggs and guards the eggs and hatchlings until they leave the nest.

MIND THE MAMBA
The green mamba lives in trees. Other mambas, such as the black mamba, live mostly on the ground. Mambas are slim, long snakes that can grow up to 4m long. Their venom is very powerful and can kill a person in only ten minutes!

DO NOT DISTURB!
The Australian mainland tiger snake is the fourth most poisonous snake in the world. It has a powerful body and smooth, shiny scales. If the tiger snake is disturbed, it puffs up its body, flattens its neck and hisses loudly. Australian tiger snakes eat almost anything, from fish and frogs to birds and small mammals.

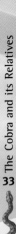

rainbow boa

CHANGING COLOURS

The rainbow boa is named after its iridescent colours, which change each time the snake moves. Light is made up of all the colours of the rainbow. When light hits the thin, see-through, outer layer of the snake's scales, it is split up into the different colours. The colours we see depend on the type of scales and the way light bounces off the scales.

COLOUR AND CAMOUFLAGE

The colours of snakes come from the pigments in the scales and from the way light reflects off the scales. Dull colours and patterns help to camouflage a snake and hide it from its enemies. The patches of colour on a snake's skin are often arranged in such a mixed-up way that the overall shape of the snake is hard to pick out. Bright colours startle and confuse predators or warn them that a snake is poisonous. Harmless snakes sometimes copy the warning colours of poisonous snakes. Dark colours may help snakes to absorb heat during cooler weather. Some female snakes become darker when they are pregnant. The extra warmth they soak up speeds up the development of the young inside their bodies. Young snakes are sometimes a different colour from their parents, but no one knows the exact reason for this.

milk snake

Did you know? Milk snakes always have the red and yellow bands between the red and yellow touching – coral snakes have black

STARTLING COLOURS

If ring-necked snakes are threatened, they show off their brightly coloured undersides to startle predators. The red tail draws attention away from the head – the most important part of the snake.

ring-necked snake

COLOUR COPIES
The bright red, yellow and black bands of this milk snake copy the colouring of the poisonous coral snake. The milk snake is not poisonous, but predators leave it alone – just in case! This colouring is found in milk snakes in the southeast of the USA. In the northeast of the USA, milk snakes are greyish with rusty blotches. There are no coral snakes in this region, so there is no point copying their warning colours.

NO COLOUR
White snakes, with no colour at all, are called albinos. People have bred some albino and other very pale snakes in captivity, out of interest. In the wild, these snakes stand out against background colours and are usually killed by predators before they can reproduce.

SNAKE MARKINGS
Like the red-tailed boa, many snakes have markings made up of patches of different colours or shades, as well as spots and stripes. These markings are usually caused by groups of different pigments in the scales.

red-tailed boa

CLEVER CAMOUFLAGE
Among the dead leaves of the rainforest floor, the gaboon viper becomes almost invisible. Many snakes have colours and patterns that match their surroundings. They usually have markings that break up their outline, so it is difficult to see where the snake ends and the background begins.

REPRODUCTION

Snakes do not live as families, and parents do not look after their young. Males and females come together to mate, and pairs may stay together for the breeding season. Most snakes are ready to mate when they are between two and five years old. In cooler climates, snakes usually mate in spring so that their young have time to feed and grow before the winter starts. Some snakes, such as garter snakes, mate after they come out of hibernation in spring, when there are a lot of snakes around. In tropical climates, snakes often mate before the rainy season, when there is plenty of food for their young. Male and female snakes usually look alike, although females are often larger than males. Male snakes find females by following their scent trails. Sometimes the males compete in a test of strength to decide who will mate with the females.

flowerpot snake

NO MATE
Scientists believe that female flowerpot snakes can produce young without males. This is useful when they move into new areas, because one snake can start a colony of snakes on its own. The problem with this type of reproduction is that all the young are the same. If conditions change, the snakes cannot adapt and may die out. When males and females mate, their characteristics get mixed up and each young snake is different. Some of these snakes may have the right characteristics to survive any changes.

FIGHTING FOR FEMALES
Rival male adders fight to test which one is the stronger. Rattlesnakes and adders often fight like this. The two males rear up and face each other, then twist their necks together. Each snake tries to push the other to the ground. In the end, one of the males gives up and crawls away.

adders

spur

SNAKE SPURS
Both boa and python males have small spurs on their bodies. These are the remains of back legs that have disappeared as snakes have developed over millions of years. A male uses its spur to scratch or tickle the female during courtship, and sometimes to fight with other males. Females may also have spurs, but they are usually smaller than the males' spurs.

Did you know? The female Javan wart snake can store sperm in her body for up to 7 years.

WRESTLING MATCH

These male Indian rat snakes are fighting to see which is the stronger. The winner will stand a better chance of mating with the females. The fight is rather like people in a wrestling match. The snakes hiss and strike out, but they seldom get hurt in these tests of strength.

SIMILARITIES AND DIFFERENCES

No one knows why the male and female of the snake shown here have such different head shapes. In fact, male and female snakes of the same species usually look similar because snakes rely on scent rather than sight to find a mate. However, differences between males and females can include eye colour, length of fangs and head shape as seen here.

male

Did you know? Some male cobras have longer fangs than the female.

Langaha nasuta

female

anacondas

MATING

Two anacondas are in the act of mating. When a female is ready to mate, she allows the male to lift her tail and coil his tail around hers. The male has to place his sperm inside the female's body to fertilize her eggs. The eggs can then develop into baby snakes. Mating lasts from a few minutes to several hours, depending on the species of the snakes.

37

Eggs

Some snakes lay eggs and some give birth to fully developed, or live, young. Egg-laying snakes include rat snakes, milk snakes, cobras, pythons and hognose snakes. A few weeks after mating, a female egg-laying snake looks for a safe, warm, moist place to lay her eggs. This may be under a rotting log, in sandy soil, under a rock or in a compost heap. The king cobra is the only snake that builds a nest. The average number of eggs laid at one time is between 6 and 30. Most snakes cover their eggs and leave them to hatch by themselves. A few snakes, such as the bushmaster, some cobras and most pythons, stay with their eggs to protect them from predators and the weather. However, once the eggs hatch, all snakes abandon their young and leave them to look after themselves.

BEACH BIRTH
A sea krait moves across the sand near an unsuspecting holidaymaker. Sea kraits are the only sea snakes to lay eggs. They often do this in caves near the sea, above the level of the salt water.

EGG CARE
This female python has piled her eggs into a pyramid shape and coiled herself around them. She does this to protect the eggs from predators. All female pythons protect their eggs. The female Indian python even twitches her muscles – rather like shivering – to warm up her body. The extra heat helps the young to develop. Snake eggs need to be kept at a certain temperature if they are to develop properly.

LAYING EGGS
The Oenpellis python lays several small eggs that have a rounded shape. Smaller snakes than pythons tend to lay fewer eggs at a time. The eggs are usually long and thin to fit inside the small body of the snake. Some snakes lay long, thin eggs when they are young, but more rounded eggs when they grow larger.

Did you know? The mud snake lays over 100 eggs at a time.

CHILDREN'S PYTHON MASS HATCHING

As they hatch, these children's pythons dent and flatten their egg shells. The shell of a snake's egg is tough and leathery, not hard and brittle like the shell of a bird's egg. Birds' eggs would break into pieces if they were squashed like this. A snake's egg is not as watertight as a bird's egg, so it has to be laid in a moist place to stop it drying up.

children's pythons

Did you know? Some snakes eat birds' eggs.

WHERE EGGS ARE LAID

Most snake eggs are white in colour. They have to be hidden in the soil, or under rocks and logs so that predators will not spot them. However, female snakes never completely bury their eggs, because the baby snakes need to breathe air that flows through the outer shell.

rat snake

HOT SPOTS

This female grass snake has laid her eggs in a pile of rotting plants. Both grass snakes and rat snakes do this. They often use compost and manure heaps. The heat given off by these heaps speeds up the development of the eggs.

HATCHING OUT

About two to four months after the adult snakes mate, the baby snakes hatch out of their eggs. Inside the egg, the baby snake feeds on the yolk, which is full of goodness. Once the snake has fully developed and the yolk has been used up, the snake is ready to hatch. Development depends on the temperature. A baby snake develops more quickly in warm climates than in colder places. All the eggs in a clutch tend to hatch at the same time. A baby snake makes slits in its shell with a sharp egg tooth. This egg tooth drops off a few hours after hatching. A few days later, the baby snake wriggles away to start a life on its own. It has to survive without any help from its parents.

1 SNAKE EGGS

Eight weeks after being laid, these rat snake eggs are beginning to hatch. While they were developing inside the egg, each baby rat snake fed on its yolk. A day or so before hatching, the yolk sac was drawn inside the snake's body. A small scar, rather like a tummy button, will show where the baby snake was once joined to the yolk.

2 STARTING TO HATCH

The baby snake has become restless, twisting inside its shell. It is now fully developed and cannot get enough oxygen through its shell. A snake's egg has an almost watertight shell, but water and gases, such as oxygen, pass in and out of it through tiny holes (pores). As the baby snake prepares to hatch, it cuts a slit in the shell with a sharp egg tooth on its snout. This egg tooth will drop off a few hours after hatching.

3 HAVING A REST

After it has broken through the stretchy shell, the baby snake has a rest. It pokes its nose through the slit in the egg to breathe the air and take a first look at the strange and exciting world outside.

4 WAITING UNTIL IT IS SAFE

All the eggs in this clutch have hatched at the same time (a clutch is a set of eggs laid by a snake). After making the first slits in their leathery shells, the baby snakes will not crawl out straight away. They poke their heads out of their eggs to taste the air with their forked tongues. If they are disturbed, they will slide back inside the shell where they feel safe. They may stay inside the shell for a few days.

Did you know? Some snakes lay as many as 100 eggs in one clutch.

5 BREAKING FREE

Eventually, the baby snake slithers out of the egg. It may be as much as seven times longer than the egg because it was coiled up inside.

Pope's tree viper

TREE BIRTH

Like most vipers, this Pope's tree viper gives birth to live young. Tree snakes often give birth high up among the branches. The clear membrane around the baby snakes sticks to the leaves and helps to prevent the baby snakes from falling out of the branches to the ground.

GIVING BIRTH

Some snakes give birth to fully developed or live young instead of laying eggs. Snakes that do this include boas, rattlesnakes, garter snakes, adders and most sea snakes. The eggs develop inside the mother's body surrounded by see-through bags, called membranes, instead of shells. While the baby snake is developing inside the mother, it gets its food from the yolk of the egg. In a few snakes, the babies take food from their mother and also pass wastes into her blood. The babies are warm and protected inside the mother, but their weight makes the mother snake heavy and slow-moving. The babies are born after a labour that may last for hours. Anything from 6 to 50 babies are born at a time. At birth, they are still inside their membranes.

BIRTH PLACE

This female sand viper has chosen a quiet, remote spot to give birth to her young. Snakes usually give birth in a safe, hidden place. They hide in underground tunnels, among rocks or logs, or in between tree roots. There, the young are safe from enemies. Water snakes and sea snakes always give birth in the water.

BABY BAGS

These red-tailed boas have just been born. They are still inside their see-through bags. The bags are made of a clear, thin, tough membrane, rather like the one inside the shell of a hen's egg.

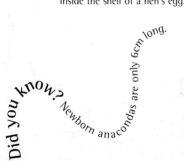

Did you know? Newborn anacondas are only 6cm long.

BREAKING FREE

This baby rainbow boa has just pushed its head through its surrounding membrane. Snakes have to break free of their baby bags on their own. The mother does not help the babies to escape. Each baby has an egg tooth to cut a slit in the membrane and wriggle out. The babies usually do this a few seconds after birth.

Did you know? Baby boa Constrictors are 30cm long when they are born.

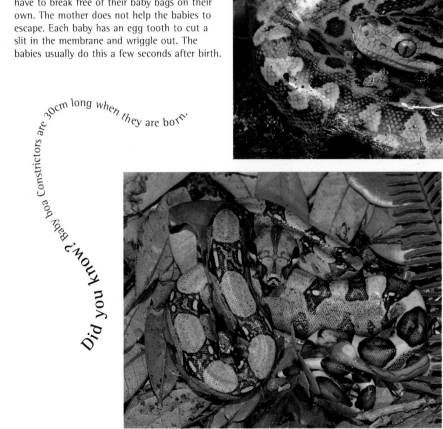

NEW BABY

A red-tailed boa has just succeeded in breaking free of its baby bag, or egg sac, which is in the front of the picture. The baby's colours are bright and shiny. Some newborn babies crawl off straight away, while others stay with their mother for a few days.

Did you know? Timber rattlesnake mothers defend their newborn babies for a few days.

COLOUR CHANGE

Believe it or not, this baby is an emerald tree boa. When young, these boas are a vivid red colour. As they grow up, they turn green. Although boas and pythons are very similar snakes in some ways, one of the principal differences between them is that boas give birth to live young while pythons lay eggs. Mother boas do not look after their young.

young emerald tree boa

GROWTH AND DEVELOPMENT

The rate at which snakes grow depends on many different things. The size when baby snakes are born or when they hatch from their eggs, how much they eat and the climate around them all affect their development. In warm climates, snakes may double or triple their length in just one year. Some snakes are mature and almost fully grown after three to five years, but slow growth may continue throughout their lives. Young snakes shed their skin more often than adults because they are growing quickly. While they are growing and developing, young snakes are easy prey for animals such as birds, racoons, toads and rats. Many rely on their camouflage colours to hide them from enemies, although poisonous snakes can defend themselves with their venom from the moment they are born.

FAST FOOD

Like all young snakes, this Burmese python must eat as much as possible in order to grow quickly. Young snakes eat smaller prey than their parents, such as ants, earthworms, flies and grasshoppers.

DEADLY BABY

This baby European adder may look tiny and harmless, but it is not! Poisonous snakes hatch out with their venom glands in full working order. They may be small, but they can give a dangerous bite soon after hatching. Luckily, the venom of the European adder is not very strong and rarely kills people.

mother European adder

baby European adder

MOTHER AND BABY

Female European adders give birth towards the end of the summer. The young adders need to grow quickly so that they will be big enough to survive the winter in hibernation. Growth stops during the hibernation period.

Burmese python

Did you know? Snakes can live for as long as 30 or 40 years.

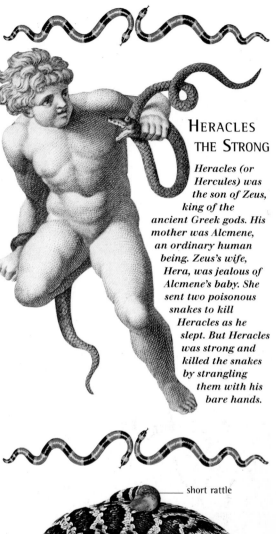

HERACLES THE STRONG

Heracles (or Hercules) was the son of Zeus, king of the ancient Greek gods. His mother was Alcmene, an ordinary human being. Zeus's wife, Hera, was jealous of Alcmene's baby. She sent two poisonous snakes to kill Heracles as he slept. But Heracles was strong and killed the snakes by strangling them with his bare hands.

DIET CHANGE
Many young Amazon tree boas live on islands in the West Indies. They change their diet as they grow up. Young Amazon tree boas start by feeding on lizards but, later on, they switch to feeding on birds and mammals.

Did you know? Female snakes reach maturity later than male snakes.

short rattle

RATTLE AGE
It is not possible to work out the age of a rattlesnake by counting the sections of its rattle. This is because several sections may be added each year and pieces of the rattle may break off.

young rattlesnake

Growth and Development

45

WHERE SNAKES LIVE

grass
snake

Snakes live on every continent except Antarctica.
They are found in most types of habitat, but are
most common in deserts and rainforests. Snakes live
in the fresh water of rivers, ponds and streams as well
as the salty water of the sea. They cannot survive in
very cold places, such as the icy polar lands or very
high mountains, because they use the heat around
them to make their bodies work. Snakes become slow
and sluggish when it gets cold and they may die if the
temperature drops too low. This is why most snakes
live in warm places where the temperature is high
enough for them to stay active day and night. In
cooler places, snakes may sleep through
the colder winter months.

GRASSLANDS
The European grass snake is one of the few
snakes to live on grasslands. There is not much
food for snakes in grasslands and not many
places to hide from predators, either.

MOUNTAINS
The Pacific rattlesnake is sometimes found
in the mountains of the western USA, often
on the lower slopes covered with loose rock.
In general, though, mountains are
problem places for snakes
because of their
cold climates.
However, some
snakes have adapted
to mountain life.
Vipers are the most common
mountain snakes.

**Pacific
rattlesnake**

WINTER SLEEP
Thousands of garter snakes emerge after their
winter sleep. In colder parts of the world, many
snakes spend the winter asleep. This is called
hibernation. Snakes often hibernate in caves or
underground, where it is warmer. In spring, the
snakes slowly come back to life.

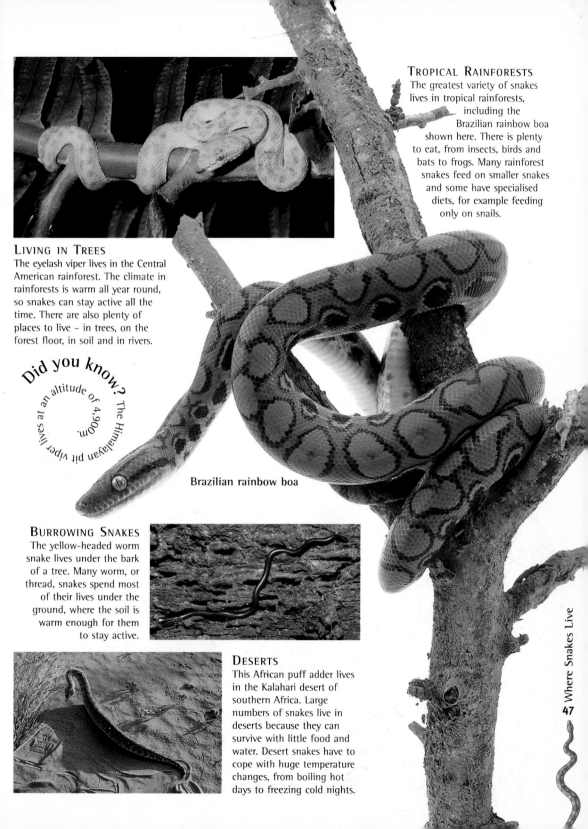

TROPICAL RAINFORESTS

The greatest variety of snakes lives in tropical rainforests, including the Brazilian rainbow boa shown here. There is plenty to eat, from insects, birds and bats to frogs. Many rainforest snakes feed on smaller snakes and some have specialised diets, for example feeding only on snails.

LIVING IN TREES

The eyelash viper lives in the Central American rainforest. The climate in rainforests is warm all year round, so snakes can stay active all the time. There are also plenty of places to live – in trees, on the forest floor, in soil and in rivers.

Did you know? The Himalayan pit viper lives at an altitude of 4,900m.

Brazilian rainbow boa

BURROWING SNAKES

The yellow-headed worm snake lives under the bark of a tree. Many worm, or thread, snakes spend most of their lives under the ground, where the soil is warm enough for them to stay active.

DESERTS

This African puff adder lives in the Kalahari desert of southern Africa. Large numbers of snakes live in deserts because they can survive with little food and water. Desert snakes have to cope with huge temperature changes, from boiling hot days to freezing cold nights.

TREE SNAKES

With their long, thin, flat bodies and pointed heads, tree snakes slide easily through the branches of tropical forests. Some can even glide from tree to tree. Most tree snakes are lightweight. Tree boas may look heavy, but they weigh less than their relatives on the ground. Tree boas and pythons have ridges on their belly scales to give them extra gripping power. Many tree snakes also have long, thin tails that coil tightly around branches. To catch prey, tree snakes use their sharp teeth or poisonous fangs. Green or brown camouflage colours keep tree snakes well hidden among the leaves and branches. They can hide from predators or lie in wait for their prey without being seen.

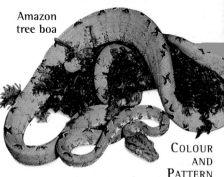

Amazon tree boa

green tree python

COLOUR AND PATTERN

This Amazon tree boa is coloured and patterned for camouflage. Many tree snakes are green or brown with patterns that break up the outline of their body shape. Some even have patterns that look like mosses and lichens.

TREE TWINS

The green tree python lives in the rainforests of New Guinea. It looks very similar to the emerald tree boa and even behaves in a similar way. But these snakes are not closely related. The emerald tree boa lives thousands of kilometres away in South America. The two snakes are similar because they both live in rainforests and both survive in the same way.

CATCHING PREY

High in the rainforests of Costa Rica, a blunt-headed tree snake has caught a lizard. Tree snakes have to grasp their prey firmly so that it does not fall out of the tree. They usually have long, sharp teeth, which are very good at piercing skin.

blunt-headed tree snake

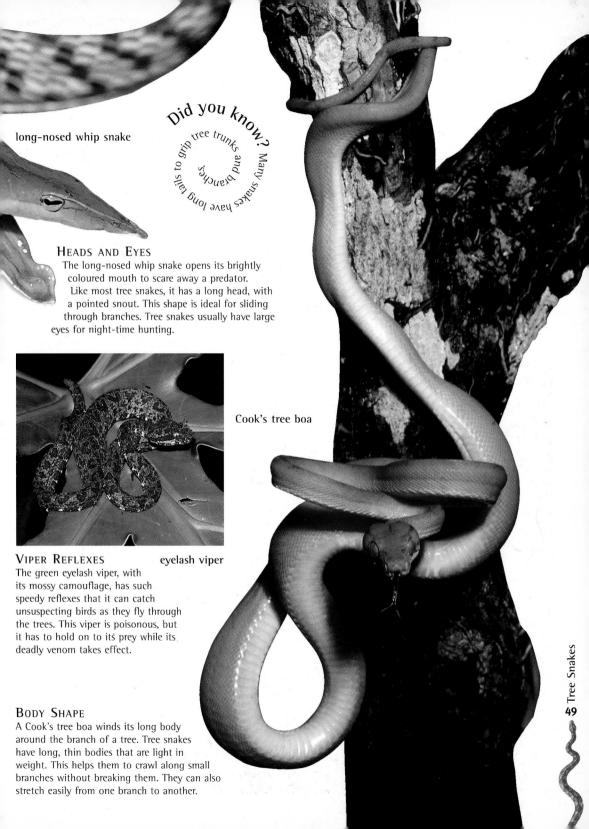

long-nosed whip snake

Did you know?
to grip tree trunks and branches. Many snakes have long tails

HEADS AND EYES

The long-nosed whip snake opens its brightly coloured mouth to scare away a predator. Like most tree snakes, it has a long head, with a pointed snout. This shape is ideal for sliding through branches. Tree snakes usually have large eyes for night-time hunting.

Cook's tree boa

VIPER REFLEXES

eyelash viper

The green eyelash viper, with its mossy camouflage, has such speedy reflexes that it can catch unsuspecting birds as they fly through the trees. This viper is poisonous, but it has to hold on to its prey while its deadly venom takes effect.

BODY SHAPE

A Cook's tree boa winds its long body around the branch of a tree. Tree snakes have long, thin bodies that are light in weight. This helps them to crawl along small branches without breaking them. They can also stretch easily from one branch to another.

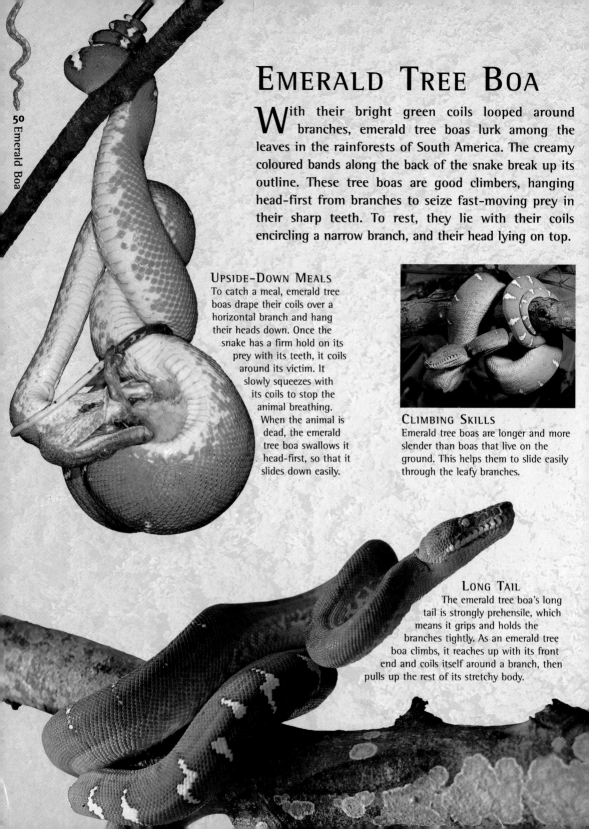

EMERALD TREE BOA

With their bright green coils looped around branches, emerald tree boas lurk among the leaves in the rainforests of South America. The creamy coloured bands along the back of the snake break up its outline. These tree boas are good climbers, hanging head-first from branches to seize fast-moving prey in their sharp teeth. To rest, they lie with their coils encircling a narrow branch, and their head lying on top.

UPSIDE-DOWN MEALS

To catch a meal, emerald tree boas drape their coils over a horizontal branch and hang their heads down. Once the snake has a firm hold on its prey with its teeth, it coils around its victim. It slowly squeezes with its coils to stop the animal breathing. When the animal is dead, the emerald tree boa swallows it head-first, so that it slides down easily.

CLIMBING SKILLS

Emerald tree boas are longer and more slender than boas that live on the ground. This helps them to slide easily through the leafy branches.

LONG TAIL

The emerald tree boa's long tail is strongly prehensile, which means it grips and holds the branches tightly. As an emerald tree boa climbs, it reaches up with its front end and coils itself around a branch, then pulls up the rest of its stretchy body.

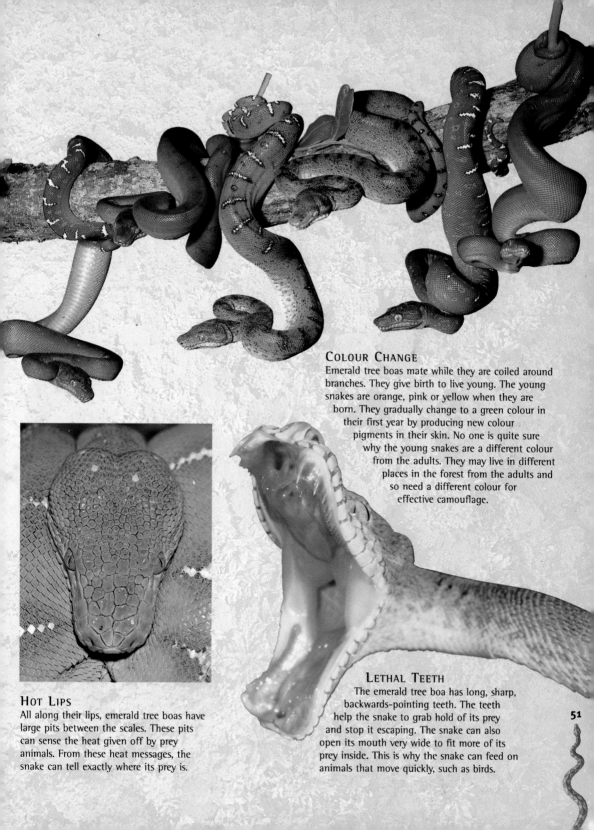

COLOUR CHANGE

Emerald tree boas mate while they are coiled around branches. They give birth to live young. The young snakes are orange, pink or yellow when they are born. They gradually change to a green colour in their first year by producing new colour pigments in their skin. No one is quite sure why the young snakes are a different colour from the adults. They may live in different places in the forest from the adults and so need a different colour for effective camouflage.

LETHAL TEETH

The emerald tree boa has long, sharp, backwards-pointing teeth. The teeth help the snake to grab hold of its prey and stop it escaping. The snake can also open its mouth very wide to fit more of its prey inside. This is why the snake can feed on animals that move quickly, such as birds.

HOT LIPS

All along their lips, emerald tree boas have large pits between the scales. These pits can sense the heat given off by prey animals. From these heat messages, the snake can tell exactly where its prey is.

DESERT SNAKES

Deserts are full of snakes. This is partly because snakes can survive for a long time without food. They don't need to use energy from their food to produce body heat because they get heat energy from their surroundings. It is also because their waterproof skins stop them losing too much water. A snake can push its long thin body between rocks or down rodent burrows to escape the fierce heat of the Sun and the bitter cold of the night. Using their special senses, such as heat pits and forked tongues, snakes can find prey at dawn or dusk, when it is cooler. Some snakes rest quietly through very hot, dry periods. They burrow deep underground, where the sand is cooler than at the surface. Then they stay there until the worst of the heat is over. This is called aestivation.

horned viper

SCALE SOUNDS

If threatened, the desert horned viper makes a loud rasping sound by rubbing together jagged scales along the sides of its body. This warns predators to keep away. If the viper hissed a warning, it would lose water into the air. Water is scarce in a desert, so a snake must keep as much water inside its body as possible.

Did you know? Most rattlesnakes live in the Southwest and Mexico.

rattlesnake

TAIL RATTLE

Rattlesnakes shake their rattle to warn enemies to keep away. The rattlesnake raises its tail to shake it and often lifts its head off the ground. The rattlesnake cannot hear the buzzing noise it makes – but its enemies can.

SAND SHUFFLE

The desert horned viper shuffles under the sand by rocking its body to and fro. It spreads its ribs to flatten the body and pushes its way down until it almost disappears. Only the eyes and horns show above the surface. The snake suddenly strikes out at its prey from this hidden position.

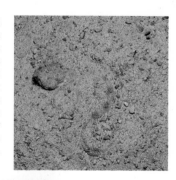

Peringuey's viper

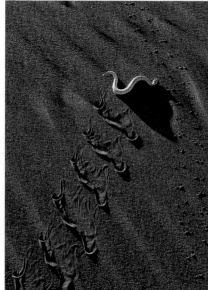

SIDEWINDING

A Peringuey's viper leaves behind a line of bar-shaped tracks as it moves across the desert sand. Many desert snakes travel in this way. It is called sidewinding. As the snake moves, only a small part of its body touches the hot sand at any one time. Sidewinding also helps to stop the snake sinking down into the loose sand.

sand boa

THE HOPI INDIANS

HIDDEN BOA

The brown and orange colours of this sand boa make it hard to spot amongst the desert rocks and sand. This helps it to hide from predators and sneak up on its prey. Sand boas have a long, round body. Their body shape helps them to burrow down into the sand.

This Native North American was a Hopi snake chief. The Hopi people used living snakes in their rain dances. They hoped the snakes would carry their prayers to the rain gods to make rain fall on their desert lands.

Desert Snakes

WATER SNAKES

Some snakes live in marshy areas or at the edge of freshwater lakes and rivers, where there is plenty of food. Two groups of snakes live in the salty water of the sea. They breathe air, but they can stay underwater for a long time. Glands on their heads get rid of some of the salt from the water. Most sea snakes give birth to their young in the water, while some have to come on to land to lay eggs. Sea snakes tend to swim in the shallow seas near the coast. They have hollow front fangs and are very poisonous. This is because a sea snake has to subdue its prey quickly in order to avoid losing it in the depths of the sea. We know very little about how sea snakes live.

sea snake

SEA SNAKE SENSES
A sea snake's eyes and nostrils are positioned towards the top of the head. This means it can take a breath without lifting its head right out of the water, and the eyes can watch out for predators about to attack from above.

CHAMPION SWIMMER
Northern water snakes are good swimmers, rarely found far from fresh water. They feed mainly on fish, frogs, salamanders and toads. At the first sign of danger, they dive under the water. Northern water snakes often bite when they are captured. Luckily, they are not poisonous.

Northern water snake

BREATH CONTROL
Most sea snakes never leave the water. When a sea snake is underwater, it can close off its nostrils to stop the water flooding in. It has a large lung that allows it to stay underwater for a few hours at a time. Only then does it have to come to the surface to breathe.

anaconda

HEAVY WEIGHT

The green anaconda lurks in swamps and slow-moving rivers, waiting for birds, turtles and caimans to come within reach of its strong coils. This one has caught a bird called an ibis. Green anacondas are the heaviest snakes in the world. They weigh up to 227 kg!

Did you know? Anacondas sometimes eat people!

sea krait

HALF AND HALF

This sea krait is crossing a sandy beach. Sea kraits are less well adapted to life in the sea than other sea snakes. Instead of giving birth in the water, they lay their eggs on land. All sea kraits have black or dark brown bands and feed on fish, particularly eels.

SNAKE FAMILIES

Scientists have divided the 2,700 different kinds of snake into about ten groups, called families. These are the colubrids, the elapids, the vipers, the boas and pythons, the sea snakes, the sunbeam snakes, the blind snakes and worm snakes, the thread snakes, the shieldtail snakes and the false coral snake. The snakes in each family have features in common. The biggest family is the colubrid family, which has over 1,800 different species of snake. Each species of snake has a Latin name that is used by scientists all over the world. This name can be used no matter what language a person speaks. A snake may have several common names, which can be confusing. But it only ever has one Latin name.

Indian cobra

Did you know?
The viper family includes rattlesnakes, adders, asps and pit vipers.

milk snake

COLUBRIDS

About three-quarters of all the snakes in the world, including this milk snake, belong to the colubrid family. They come in almost every shape, size or colour. Most colubrids are not poisonous. Colubrids have no left lung or hip bones, and their heads are covered with large, symmetrical scales.

VIPERS   sand viper

Snakes in this family, such as the sand viper, have long, hollow fangs that can be folded back inside the mouth when they are not needed. Vipers are usually short, with thick bodies and wide heads. Their scales have heavy ridges, or keels.

ELAPIDS

Elapids are poisonous snakes that live in hot countries around the world. They include cobras in Asia and Africa, mambas in Africa and coral snakes in the Americas. All the poisonous snakes of Australia are elapids, such as the tiger snake, king brown snake and the taipan. Elapids have short, fixed fangs at the front of their mouths.

CLASSIFICATION CHART		
	Kingdom	Animalia
	Phylum	Chordata
	Class	Reptilia
	Order	Squamata
	Suborder	Ophidia
	Family	Boidae
	Genus	Boa
	Species	Boa constrictor

This chart shows how a boa constrictor is classified within the animal kingdom.

Colombian
rainbow boa

BOAS AND PYTHONS

This family
includes snakes
that kill by
constriction rather than
poisoning. They have curved
teeth, hip bones and tiny back leg
bones. Most boas live in Central and South
America, whereas pythons live in Africa,
Southeast Asia and Australia.

SEA SNAKES

The family of sea snakes includes some snakes
that are born in the sea and spend all their
lives there, and others that spend part of their
time on land. Sea snakes have flattened tails
for swimming and nostrils that can be closed
off under the water. Most live in warm waters,
from the Red Sea to New Zealand and Japan.
No sea snakes live in the Atlantic Ocean. Sea
snakes are sometimes grouped together
with the elapid family.

sea snake

sunbeam snake

SUNBEAM SNAKES

The sunbeam snake family has only two
members. The name of the sunbeam snake
comes from the way its scales reflect the light.
Sunbeam snakes are burrowing snakes that live
in Southeast Asia and southern China. Unlike
most other snakes, they have two working
lungs, although the left lung is about half the
size of the right lung.

Did you know? Some scientists put pythons and boas into different families.

sand lizard

LIZARDS
This sand lizard is threatening an enemy by making itself look big and frightening. Lizards usually have four legs, feet with sharp claws and a long tail. They also have movable eyelids and good eyesight. Most lizards have pointed tongues, but monitor lizards have a forked tongue.

SNAKE RELATIVES

Snakes are part of a large group of animals called reptiles. There are about 6,000 different kinds of reptiles alive today, nearly half of which are snakes. Other reptiles include lizards, crocodiles and alligators, turtles and tortoises. Reptiles have bony skeletons with a backbone and bodies covered in scales. They lay eggs with waterproof shells or give birth to live young. Young reptiles look like tiny copies of their parents. Reptiles are cold-blooded and rely on their surroundings for heat, so they live mostly in warm places. Snakes appeared on the Earth more recently than other reptiles. The first snakes lived between 100 and 150 million years ago, alongside the most famous reptiles of all – the dinosaurs.

Did you know? The largest reptile in the world is the saltwater crocodile, which grows over 7m long.

baby crocodile

CARING CROCODILES
Crocodiles are some of the largest and most dangerous living reptiles. Yet female crocodiles make doting mothers. They stand guard over their eggs and protect their young until they are old enough to fend for themselves.

LEGLESS LIZARDS

Some burrowing lizards, including skinks, have long, snake-like bodies and very short legs – or no legs at all. Snakes possibly developed from burrowing lizards, which did not need legs for sliding through the soil or leaf litter.

legless lizard

Did you know?
The only two poisonous lizards are the gila monster and the Mexican beaded lizard.

LIZARD TAILS

Lizards, like this water dragon, generally have long tails and shed their skin in several pieces. Some lizards can grow a new tail if their tail breaks off in a fight with a predator.

water dragon

TORTOISES

A tortoise has a shell as well as a skeleton inside its body. The shell is made from bony plates fused to the ribs, with an outer covering of horny plates. It is useful for protection, but it is also very heavy. The tortoise's long neck can be drawn right back inside its shell.

tortoise

WORM LIZARDS

These strange reptiles are fierce predators that look rather like earthworms. Worm lizards live underground, digging burrows with their strong, hard heads. Their nostrils point backwards and they close during burrowing so that they do not get clogged up with soil.

worm lizard

Snake Relatives

CONSERVATION

The biggest threat to snakes comes from people. Some snakes are killed because people are afraid of them. Farmers often kill snakes to protect their farm animals and workers, although many snakes actually help farmers by eating pests. In some countries, people catch snakes for food or use parts of their bodies to make medicines. Snake skins are also used to cover expensive jewellery, shoes, belts and bags. Snakes are sometimes captured and sold as exotic pets. Also, when people move into an area, snakes' habitats are often destroyed. To help snakes survive, people need to learn more about them and take action to preserve their habitats, so that they have safe places in which to live.

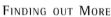

FINDING OUT MORE

These scientists are tracking a black-tailed rattlesnake in Arizona, USA. They use an antenna to pick up radio signals from a transmitter fitted to the snake. This allows them to follow the snake's movements even when they cannot see it. There are still many gaps in our knowledge about snakes. The more we know about how they live, the easier it is to protect them.

TROPHY

Although snakes are killed for food in some parts of the world, there are unfortunately still those who shoot them for recreation. As a trophy demonstrating their sporting achievements, the hunters put the rattles or head of the snake on display.

SNAKES IN DANGER

Snakes such as this Dumeril's boa are in danger of dying out altogether if people do not do something to save them. Laws can be passed to stop collectors taking snakes from the wild, but it is difficult to make sure people obey the law. Other threats to snakes are more difficult to solve, such as people building roads or towns in places where snakes live.

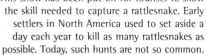

This show has been put on for tourists to show the skill needed to capture a rattlesnake. Early settlers in North America used to set aside a day each year to kill as many rattlesnakes as possible. Today, such hunts are not so common.

USING SNAKE SKINS

Snake skins have been used for many years to make bracelets and earrings such as these. Certain snake skins are more popular than others, and some species have declined as a result of intensive killing for skins in some areas. Recently, countries such as Sri Lanka and India have banned the export of snake skins.

Did you know? Legend says St Patrick banished snakes from Ireland to rid the country of evil.

PET SNAKES

Some people like to keep pet snakes. However, they do not do very much and are not happy in captivity. Snakes can lose the ability to hunt and dislike being kept in a confined space.

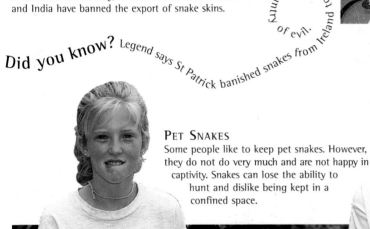

61 Conservation

GLOSSARY

A

aestivation
A period of rest during heat and drought, similar to hibernation.

albino
An animal that has no colour on all or part of its body but belongs to a species that is usually coloured.

anaconda
A type of boa.

antivenin
A substance made from the blood of mammals and/or snake venom that is used to treat snakebite.

B

boas
A group of snakes that live mainly in North and South America. They kill by constriction and give birth to live young.

brille
A transparent scale covering a snake's eye. It is also called a spectacle.

C

camouflage
Colours or patterns that allow a snake to blend in with its surroundings.

classification
Grouping of animals according to their similarities and differences in order to study them. This also suggests how they may have developed over time.

cloaca
Combined opening of the end of the gut, the reproductive system and the urinary system in reptiles, amphibians and birds.

clutch
The number of eggs laid by a female at one time.

cobras
Poisonous snakes in the elapid family, with short, fixed fangs at the front of the mouth.

cold-blooded
An animal whose temperature varies with that of its surroundings.

colubrids
Mostly harmless snakes. These snakes make up the biggest group –nearly three-quarters of the world's snakes.

compost heap
A pile of layers of garden plants, leaves and soil. Compost gives off heat as it rots down and can eventually be dug into the soil to make it rich. This helps plants to grow.

constrictor
A snake that kills by coiling its body tightly around its prey to suffocate it.

D

digestion
The process of absorbing food into the stomach and bowels.

E

ectotherm
A cold-blooded animal.

egg tooth
A small tooth sticking out of the mouth of snake hatchlings, which is used to slit open the egg.

elapids
A group of poisonous snakes that includes the cobras, mambas and the coral snakes. Elapids live in hot countries.

epidermis
The outer layer of the skin.

F

fang
A long, pointed tooth that may be used to deliver venom.

H

hibernation
A period of rest during the winter when body processes slow down.

J

Jacobson's organ
Nerve pits in the roof of a snake's mouth into which the tongue places scent particles.

K

keratin
A horny substance that makes up a snake's scales.

M

mature
Developed enough to be capable of reproduction.

membrane
A thin film, skin or layer.

moulting
The process by which a snake sheds its skin.

P

pigment
Colouring

pits
Heat sensors located on either side of a snake's head.

predator
A living thing that catches and kills other living things for food.

prey
An animal that is hunted by animals or by people for food.

python
A group of snakes that lives mainly in Australia, Africa and Asia. Pythons kill their prey by constriction. They lay eggs.

R

rainforest
A tropical forest where it is hot and wet all year round.

rattlesnakes
Snakes that live mainly in the south-west United States and Mexico. They have a warning rattle made of empty tail sections at the end of the tail.

S

saliva
A colourless liquid produced by glands in the mouth. Saliva helps to slide food from the mouth to the throat. In some snakes, saliva also aids digestion.

spurs
Leg bones attached to the hip bones, which are found in boas and pythons and used during courtship displays.

V

venom
Poisonous fluid produced in the glands of some snakes to kill their prey.

vipers
A group of very poisonous snakes with fangs that fold. Some vipers have heat pits on their faces. Most vipers give birth to live young.

W

warm-blooded
An animal (such as a mouse or a human being) that is able to maintain its body at roughly the same temperature all the time.

warning colours
Bright colours that show others that an animal is poisonous. Bright colours also warn predators to keep away.

windpipe
The tube leading from the mouth to the lungs. It is through this that an animal takes in fresh air (containing oxygen) and gives out used air (containing carbon dioxide).

Y

yolk
Food material that is rich in protein and fats. It nourishes a developing embryo inside an egg.

INDEX

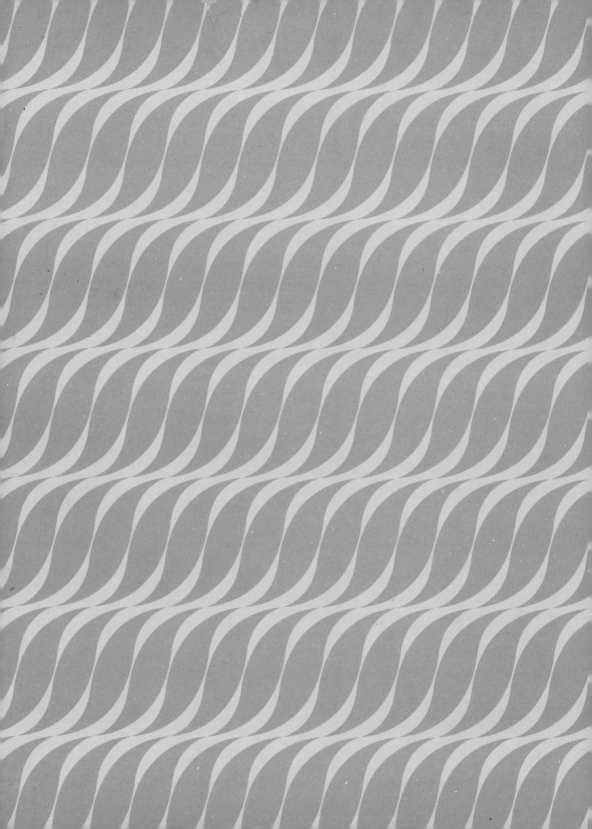